RIDE
AT YOUR
OWN RISK

True Rideshare Stories

Written by
Darci Dexter

Title: Ride At Your Own Risk
Author: Darci Dexter
Illustrations: Evgeny Bychkov
Layout and Cover Page Design: Anastasia Ognev

ISBN: 978-0-578-80651-8

Website: www.darcidexter.com
Email: ride@darcidexter.com

Be My Stranger, I'll Be Your Driver

Dedication

I would like to dedicate this book to the nearly apocalyptic year of 2020. The year of extremes, uncertainty, and change. The year that stopped time, giving us a chance to get to know ourselves better and do what we love. Moreover, the year serving as a rollercoaster moving ahead in a fast-paced motion creating violence, hoax, and confusion.

This book is written proof that there IS hope in us. There IS a way to start appreciating each other's differences, to listen, learn, understand, and to evolve into better human beings. It all starts with paying attention to each other with open hearts leaving judgment aside.

I would like to take a moment and thank the universe for putting all the obstacles and people on my path that made this book possible. All my passengers with their own unique stories. There are no two people, life stories or experiences the same. But I can assure you—there is one thing we ALL have in common. We are all human and want to be happy.

A special thank you goes to my husband for being my best friend and number one supporter in everything I do. Thank you for your wisdom and inspiration, and for always being there for me. Also, our three boys—thank you guys for never questioning my choices, supporting, encouraging, and loving unconditionally.

Love you all!

Table Of Contents

Chapter 1.

"What Is Rideshare?"

*"You have to learn the rules of the game.
And then, you have to play better than anyone else."*

~ Albert Einstein ~

A fter almost two years of driving for a well-known rideshare company (from here on "Rideshare"), I still ask myself the same questions. Was Rideshare really invented to only support our commutes? What if there is so much more behind sharing rides in the era of technology and rapid progress of everything else but one—communication on a simple human level?

What if the Universe has a plan that is so much more than just going back and forth in all different directions?

How come we are put together with a complete stranger for a certain amount of time, which expires like a ticking timer in front of our eyes? How do we use this time? How do we treat each other? Why?

We all are so different with distinctive life experiences, opinions, and backgrounds. We all have different energy and frequency levels that let us achieve certain goals differently. *What if we are finally mixed up together to exchange all that we have been through and to learn from each other?*

The way Rideshare is created, from a driver's seat it is an endless race to please and to do better, be a nicer and more helpful person or you are going to be judged. It can be quite exhausting. At the end of the day you understand, you can get out of your own skin to care, but you are never going to be good enough for everybody. *There are forces above us, a lot more powerful, knowing exactly which people need to be sent our way and what situations we should be put in to experience all the diversity of different human natures. It doesn't matter if we understand it or not, there is a reason beyond what we think at first. It is to create a better version of us that is meant to come out of a certain experience.*

Without any doubt, Rideshare is one of the all times greatest inventions. A unique business model of an invisible middleman between its servants and customers. Can we call it an employer? Theoretically, yes, but practically it has its own understanding of liabilities and responsibilities towards the drivers and the passengers that the best word to describe what Rideshare is—a game.

The game called Rideshare, with a small print disclaimer "Ride at Your Own Risk." A game sounds a lot more suitable for the system developed to protect the invisible middleman, amazingly smart, and technologically developed "monster" with many hands pulling the strings attached to each individual player of the game.

If you are at the end of the driver's string, make sure that you read the rules and play by them or your string is going to be pulled. You are going to be judged and eventually punished. But then again, you can play by the rules and be the best player in the game until some other player (a rider) cheats or simply does not know the rules. To your big surprise, no one else's string is going to be pulled but yours again!

You probably know how it feels to be wrongly accused without a chance to defend yourself. Wronged not just once but continuously for a long period of time. Then you should also know the need to explain your side of the story. The truth is if you drive for Rideshare you cannot defend yourself. Why? Because there is no one who is going to listen, no one who cares, and your "rightness" would not change a thing in the big game.

Let me give you an example here. Everyone who is a player of Rideshare, is familiar with the term Pool, right? (Note: *This riding option was removed in 2020 due to the virus outbreak to lessen contact between unrelated passengers*). We all know that there are certain rules that apply to this type of service that all involved players must comply with. Then there is another term—Express Pool. For some reason, the rules of this option are poorly explained or the players (riders) think that it is in their power to change these rules.

So, when it is time to finish an Express Pool ride and let the passenger out, most of the times it is at the spot where Rideshare map finds it the most convenient in order to continue the ride with other passengers. It is rarely the exact location an Express Pool rider has marked as their drop-off location.

Here is where the conflict starts, when the rider would like to go against the rules and blame the driver for a wrong drop-off location. However, all the driver sees is a red dot in the middle of the ride.

Now, the driver stops, the passenger gets out and rates the driver a one star with a comment about unprofessional navigation, thinking that this way he has served his justice to protect his rights.

What do you think happens next? The big monster pulls his string with this particular driver attached saying "Bad boy (girl)! I received a complaint: you did not follow the main rule to keep my customer happy. You are being punished—your overall rating is dropping, and you are one step closer to losing your benefits."

Speaking of the middleman, string "monster," aka Rideshare—how does it look? Seriously, does anyone have a clear vision (even blurred) who is behind this everyday necessity that has become almost as important as food and air that we breathe?

There is a support phone number for small issues like "missing trip information" or "cannot get online" type of problems. When you call that number, you certainly take a quick time-traveling trip to a different country, and John politely answers with an extremely heavy accent calling you by your name and asking how he can help.

Whoever John and all other customer service reps on the phone are, they have very little to no understanding of what driving for Rideshare really means because they cannot relate to everyday situations. Nevertheless, they are well trained to be overly polite and apologetic to the point that it can drive you insane. These people have their strings attached to the same monster. In my vision, these strings are noticeably short without any value and if broken,  thrown out along with the attachments—no questions asked.

Oh, almost forgot, there is a customer service center for drivers in Chicago. God forbid, if you must go there, let's say to pick up a document or a sticker, you are treated as if they own you. They have no idea how it is done, yet they are quick to tell you their opinion. Any time that I have asked a rep if they have ever driven for Rideshare, the answer has always been "no."

Now tell me, would you go to a "specialist" who calls himself a dentist but has never touched anyone else's teeth but his own? Would you trust a shoemaker who cannot differentiate a leather from pleather? How about someone who calls himself a cook but the only experience he has had is with mixing ingredients to make rat poisoning?

I think you have a full picture of a list that could become very long. *How can someone who has never done what you are doing give you advice on how to do it better?* In my opinion, as part of their skill requirement, they should complete at least 100 mandatory rides before they can be hired as customer service reps.

Anyways, Rideshare has been loved and hated by many, discussed, and analyzed by experts and amateurs, tried to be copied, prohibited, and restricted. There are no winners or losers in this game. If played by the rules—everybody involved should benefit, especially the one and only—multi-handed monster itself.

Long story short. The game has been invented; the rules have been set. In a fantasy game or in life—if you want to play the game, you must learn and follow the rules, or you will get eliminated. The better you know the rules, the more chances of winning you have!

In the Rideshare game there are general rules and then there are rules that you set for yourself. Those are the most important ones. Those are the rules that let you keep your rating high, earn promotions, recognitions, and tips.

Chapter 2.

"Highly-Rated Drivers
Have Told Us..."

*"The greatest mistake you can make in life is
to be continually fearing you will make one."*

~ Elbert Hubbard ~

There is a certain message that appears on a driver's app in each specific case of "misbehaving." For instance, the rider was not able to find the ride right at the door front where he came out, he rated the driver one star and complained in a comment.

Regardless of the comment, Rideshare will post for the driver the following feedback:

 "Pickup experience. Riders may give this feedback if they had trouble coordinating their pickup with you. **Highly-rated drivers have told us** they always go straight to the rider's pick-up location and call the rider if they have trouble finding them."

Really sorry to hear that. However, little this rider has been educated that by dropping the pin at his preferred pick-up location or using a "current location" option might not be precise and mislead the driver where to look for the rider.

"Highly rated drivers have told us..." Well, my rating is 4.99 stars. No one has ever asked my opinion on what I do in a certain situation. That is why I am trying hard to work up to that missing 0.01 stars hoping that my opinion will finally matter.

I hope you heard the sarcastic tone in my voice when I said that. As I mentioned before, you cannot possibly be good for everybody, and you should not really care too much or you might lose your sanity.

Here is another bit of feedback:

 "Driving. Some riders may be more sensitive to hard braking or interpret speeding up to make a yellow light differently. **Highly-rated drivers**

follow our Community Guidelines, which outline the importance of sticking to the rules of the road"

Clearly, this passenger (or whoever came up with this message) had never been behind the steering wheel of a car. For those who drive, it is not necessary to explain that there are many different situations on the roads. Most likely, the driver made the best decision in a given situation either it was to break hard and stop or to speed up and cross the intersection even if it was a yellow light. Then if the passenger was taken to his destination safe and sound, he should be nothing but thankful.

Another "valuable" piece of feedback:

"Comfort. While riders may have different preferences when it comes to the comfort of your car, **highly-rated drivers have found** it helpful to ask riders how they want the temperature set, and if they have enough legroom."

Let me tell you a big secret that I have found out from my highly-rated passengers. If they are cold or hot, they ASK if the temperature could be adjusted. And guess what happens next?

The temperature gets adjusted to their comfort level! Yay!

(Shhhh... Just do not tell anyone. Remember, it is a secret.)

Honestly, with all due respect, I cannot even imagine how oversized someone must be not to have enough legroom in a crew cabin of a pickup truck. Well...

Whoever these passengers are who complain to Rideshare about their "issues," the driver never finds out who that was and what he or she was complaining about. Those complaints are worthless because the driver has no idea what exactly he or she had done wrong. There are so many people they give rides to that they cannot possibly know who in particular was not pleased to their expectations.

These "informative" Rideshare tips do not solve and certainly do not improve the quality of the service. They only stir up an unpleasant feeling of unfairness because to improve I must know what I have done wrong.

This is the most recent feedback with one-star rating in addition:

"Navigation apps are helpful, but some riders are particular about the route they like to take. Feel free to ask riders if they have a preferred route. **5-star drivers** familiarize themselves with their city to make their own decisions about the best route to take."

Well...

"... familiarize themselves with their city to make their own decisions." Wait, what? Why? If they have those riders with their preferred routes in mind, then how in the world these 5-star drivers allow themselves to make their own decisions? Whoever wrote this "valuable" teaching should read it one more time and to rewrite it so that it would make sense.

Riders—if you have a preferred "secret" route in mind it is OK to share it with your driver. He or she is not going to tell your "secret desires" to anyone but use it to take you where you need to go.

"Navigation apps are helpful"—actually they are the only reliable source to take you from a point A to a point B. Usually, the passengers with the most requests "turn left," "turn right" end up wasting their own time the most. So often, there was road construction they did not know about or other obstacles that end up making the trip even longer.

Listen to this pearl:

> Service quality. When riders give feedback about service quality, they are letting you know that the service they received was not what they expected. Each rider is unique and may have different expectations, but **highly-rated drivers tell us** they are polite and keep the conversation away from sensitive subject matters.

Without comments, straight to the apologies to all mama's boys and daddy's little girls. "Sorry, guys, for not being polite and for not keeping the conversation away from sensitive subjects. I don't know who you are, but just in case, you are one of them, my sincere apology goes to you too!"

I just wonder who are those highly-rated drivers that get everything right? Maybe Rideshare should pull all strings together and hold a meeting for not-so-highly-rated drivers? The ones who don't go straight to the pickup location, don't call their riders if they can't find them, who always break hard and speed up to make a yellow light, keep their passengers either frozen or sweating with no leg room, who are rude and choose especially sensitive subjects to talk

about. All that while driving their passengers around purposefully ignoring their preferred routes and making decisions to take the worst possible roads available.

Once you learn that even by being the best version of yourself you cannot possibly please everybody, everything becomes so simple and easy. The only thing you should be concentrating on is to do what makes YOU happy. Surprisingly only then the right people start entering your life and the right events begin occurring. Where "right" refers to—what is best for YOU.

Rules are rules but use your common sense to follow them.

In life and in the Rideshare game—you cannot be afraid of a judgement or you are not going to get anywhere. There are so many people who are not happy with themselves and who would want everybody else to feel miserable. Do not live up to their expectations, they are in charge of their own "business" and they have to "pay" for it, not adding to your expenses.

Chapter 3.

"You Can Do It!"

*"You'll never do a whole lot unless
you're brave enough to try."*

~ Dolly Parton ~

I am a tall, blond girl (well, based on my experience, maybe you'd say "tall blond woman"), full of life, positivity, and readiness to serve.

I am a designer and a business owner, a former teacher of art and psychology, media specialist, social media account developer, and personal growth mentor. A wife and a mother. In short, I love what I do, and I do what I love. The sky is the limit, and one day I decided to try something new.

Like in the movie about the game called Jumanji, I was sucked into a game called Rideshare.

At the time I started driving for Rideshare, I was a proud owner of a big black custom-built, pickup truck, Ford F-150. Why such choice of a vehicle, you might ask? It was the vehicle for the business my husband and I owned. The truck was my only four-door car option at that time, so I took it as a challenge not knowing what I was getting myself into. My husband was teasing me "There is no way you are going to do it," which gave me even more courage! Tell me not to do something, and I will do it twice and take pictures!

This is where I was before my Rideshare journey. I wanted to know how Rideshare works and how I could benefit from it.

Very soon, I started shocking my passengers daily every time I arrived in a truck. It was a good first shock followed by the second shock when they opened the door. "Oh, a woman is driving!" As if they did not see my face in the app before I arrived. I do not blame them though because if I did not know me, I would not combine those three together either—a woman, a truck, and Rideshare.

The truck played a major role in my self-learning experience along the way. Judgment, excitement, excessive interest, surprise, doubt, and confidence were just some of the emotions that served as instant icebreakers and subject to keep conversations going.

So, here it comes, the very first time. On a random afternoon, driving home from our business, I decided to finally do IT. I was putting off this moment for a while, dragging out the idea in my thoughts for days.

"You can do it!" I finally told myself and pressed the "GO" button in the Rideshare app. Little did I know how it works and what would happen next. I had no idea what journey I set myself up for in August of 2017. How long was it going to last and what was it going to teach me?

I did not have to wait long for my phone to start making a strange beeping sound with a turning circle on the bottom of the screen.

"Oh, I guess that's my first passenger!" I said to myself and started to chase the circle with my finger to make it stop.

"Ha, I got it!"

"Jennifer (the name of my first passenger), please be patient. I am on my way!" I said it aloud. "Yeah, just let me figure out what to press next in the app to find you." Hmmm, it did not take that long, very proud of myself!

As I was approaching the Hilton hotel in Rosemont, I had a feeling this might be MY Jennifer with two other ladies waiting outside for their ride.

Not only had I shocked them by arriving in a pickup truck, but I also greeted them with a "Hello, Ladies! You are my first passengers! Please, forgive me just in case something goes wrong."

They were extremely supportive, understanding, cheerful, and chatty. At some point, I felt like all four of us were in a driver's seat. Jennifer said, "This is the coolest ride I have ever had! Good luck with all the next rides to come!" Before they left, I was complimented on my truck, appearance, and a laid-back personality, promised to be given five stars rating and a tip. "Thank you, Ladies! Have a good day!" I said as they were getting out of my truck.

"Awesome," I thought. "This seems to be a good start! If so, I can do it!" Little did I know a "start" to what exactly it was.

Alright! Ready? Buckle up and make yourself comfortable in the seat of my pickup truck, I will take you for a ride and show around! I will tell you some great Rideshare stories and discuss the lessons learned.

Disclaimer*** RIDE AT YOUR OWN RISK

Chapter 4.

"No. It Is Your Job"

*"There is a fountain of youth: it is your mind,
your talents, the creativity you bring to your life and
the lives of people you love. When you learn to tap
this source, you will truly have defeated age."*

~ Sophia Loren ~

A fter about a month of giving rides, I was put in this interesting situation. A middle-aged woman called Rideshare for her old mother to be taken to her weekly doctor's checkup at the hospital. I arrived in my big truck. The woman was already outside, getting ready to leave in her car to take her son to the airport. She approached me, opened the passenger side door, trying to evaluate if her mom would make it in. We had a nice conversation, and I openly offered to cancel the ride to make sure that she doesn't get charged and she could call another car if she felt like her mom would not be able to get in.

The woman said, "No, no, I want my mom to go with you. She is already coming out."

"Okay, of course! I will gladly take her where she needs to go," I replied.

I saw an old lady with a cane slowly moving into the direction of my truck. She was noticeably overweight, and I could see by the way she was walking that she was in pain. Her daughter went to help her.

I got out of the driver's seat and walked around the truck to open the door for her.

I could hear the old lady complaining, "I do not want to go anywhere. How am I going to get in? How am I going to get out? "

Her daughter was comforting her by saying, "She is really nice; she will help you to get out."

The daughter decided that it is better for her mom to sit in the front seat, as it looked like a better option to get in and out. While opening the front door for the old lady, I offered one more time to cancel the ride for no charge so that they can call another car.

The daughter abruptly repeated, "No, I want my mother to go with you."

What I saw next was quite entertaining. Poor old lady tried to pull herself up to get into the truck while using the step. (Note: *For those who have never been in a truck I will explain that a pick-up truck is a lot higher than a regular sedan or even SUV, so there is an extra step outside that you have to use to get in)* While doing it she kept complaining and was clearly resisting getting in.

What followed next made me smile—the daughter started pushing her mom in from behind. I was surprised at the strengths the daughter had to finally get her mother in the front seat of my truck. There must be a serious reason behind her strengths and determination that I learned all about it in the following forty-five minutes...

I got back into the driver's seat. The daughter said, "Thank you very much." She closed the door and we were ready to start the ride.

The old lady was sitting next to me so miserable and unhappy, I wanted to comfort her by saying that I will take good care of her and help whatever she needs help with. While saying that, I put my hand on her slightly shaking hand that she tried to keep still on the cover of the middle compartment section that was separating me from her. She rapidly pulled her hand out and said nothing.

Fine. I guess I should not worry that much.

We started driving and soon entered the expressway heading towards downtown Chicago. The traffic was close to a standstill and GPS showed a forty-five-minute ride to the hospital.

I do not know why it took so long but her unbuckled seatbelt suddenly started to remind about itself by making loud beeping noise. I waited one round of beeps to end and asked her nicely if she could put her seat belt on.

"No. It is your job," she replied without any hesitation.

At first, I thought that she was joking, but then I understood that she was not going to do it. If we were on a road where I could stop, I would help her. I would have to get out of the truck, go to her side and buckle her up. As we were on the highway, I politely said "Sorry, I really can't help you in this situation."

The loud beeping did not stop as we kept driving.

As we drove, the old lady showed her true nature. She started complaining about everything! "What is wrong with this traffic? Why are you driving is this lane? Why is this taking so long? How long have you been driving?"

"For Rideshare?" I asked.

"How long how you been driving?" she repeated.

"A month," I confirmed.

"Oooooh. That explains it all..." she said and turned her head to the right so that she did not have to see the traffic congestion ahead and possibly me on the left. Did she think that my total driving ex-

35

perience was one month? Who knows, and honestly, I did not want to find out her thoughts on any topic.

A few minutes of silence and then it all continued: the loud beeping sound, along with my grumpy passenger complaining. This time she chose a wider range of topics to complain about—her daughter who did not care about her, her health issues, and her bad life, in general.

I had wondered why her daughter did not take her mom to the hospital and have Rideshare drive her son to go to the airport. After just the first twenty minutes with this woman, I got the answer without having to ask. The funny scene of her daughter pushing her mom into my truck suddenly made so much sense. The daughter had demonstrated superhuman strength just to send her mother away with a complete stranger who seemed to be caring enough and compassionate to help her mother, if needed. And you know what—I didn't blame her one bit!

We finally got to the main entrance of the medical building.

"I'll help you to get out," I offered to my passenger.

"No. Go inside and ask the staff to help me." She made it clear that I was not good enough.

As I was walking inside, the automated sliding door opened wide so that everybody at the front desk along with two security officers could see outside and recognize who had arrived. I saw smiles on their faces, and I did not have to say anything as one of the officers asked if SHE needs help.

"Yes, please." I felt like they all knew her.

"I am really sorry that you had to go through this," the officer said as we were walking towards the truck. I looked at him surprised, not sure if he really knew what I was just through with this lady.

"Everybody here knows her. She has been coming here for years. We are glad to help her in but, oh boy, how happy we are to help her out!" he was joking, still trying to remain respectful towards the patient of the clinic he was working for.

He helped my grumpy passenger to get out of the truck and gave me a thumbs up.

Oh, my! How happy I was THAT ride was over! As I was leaving that place, I rolled all four windows down so that the breeze of fresh air could blow in and erase the memory of this ride.

This felt like one of those movies where you can see two different outcomes. I saw the worst outcome, what someone becomes living life with negative thoughts and blaming everybody else instead of being in charge of their lives to make it better while it is still in their power.

Knowing the worst, I can create the best for myself! Universe, please do not let me become someone like this old grumpy grandma; lead me through life so that I stay loving and likable person! I do not want to be pushed from behind in a pickup truck and sent away with a stranger.

Chapter 5.

"Wasted, I'm On These Drugs, I Feel Wasted"

"It is not our differences that divide us.
It is our inability to recognize, accept,
and celebrate those differences."

~ Audre Lorde ~

*A*t first, I would classify this as just another regular day of driving around in my pickup truck and serving people of Chicago. In exchange, becoming a little part of their busy lives, listening to their stories, and "taking a walk in their shoes." Also, and most importantly, learning my own valuable lessons.

It was a beautiful, sunny Tuesday afternoon. Uncontrollably, ride by ride, I was taken out of my way and far from where I would normally drive, about 40 miles away from downtown Chicago. It always hits you hard when you realize that you are in the middle of nowhere, in a suburb that you never knew existed and that you must get back to where you started.

I set up the destination mode in the Rideshare app, hoping to get a passenger that needed to go where I wanted to go, which in this case, was home. To my big surprise, I did not have to wait long. (Thank you, Rideshare, for understanding and support!)

"Yay!" I was excited as there was somebody by name Andre who needed me as much as I needed him!

As I was driving closer to where I had to pick him up, I saw somebody with long dreadlocks standing outside, holding a backpack in one hand and a cigarette in the other. He was nervously trying to get as much smoke as he could before getting into the truck.

"Can I finish my cigarette, please?" He opened the back door and asked politely.

"Well... OK... Fine..." I mumbled while processing all the thoughts running through my mind with a speed of 1000 miles per hour. I cannot stand the smell of smoke. What can be worse than the last exhale of a second-hand smoke before getting into my truck? Yuck! I was so close to canceling this ride. But then, I remembered that I am in the middle of nowhere and that he was sent to get me out of here.

He threw his backpack inside, on the back seat and closed the door, staying outside to finish his cigarette.

"What? Did I smell it right?" I said it aloud to myself. It was not a cigarette that he was smoking. It was weed...

Seriously! I was frustrated with the whole situation even more. There is no way he is getting into my truck! But then again that little voice in my head was reminding me that I needed him to get out of here...

"Thank you!" He said politely as he opened the door and got into the truck. "I should probably open the window." Andre continued obviously feeling uncomfortable as I was looking at him in silence, still fighting my inner "get out of here" and "let's go" commands.

"I would say, you MUST open the window, maybe even all windows," I said as firm as I could, making sure that he understood how disappointed I was.

We started driving with all four windows down. The smell was still strong and at that point, I did not want to be responsible for the worst possible consequences in case we would be pulled over. "No, I simply cannot do this. The smell is disgusting," I told him and stopped the truck expecting him to get out. (Note: *This ride took place before marijuana was legalized in Illinois.*)

"I do this occasionally because of the stage fright. I have to perform tonight in an audition, and this is the only way I can get over anxiety and to relax. If you want me to get out, I will. I apologize for making you feel uncomfortable," he said quietly, respectfully and as always politely.

"What stage? What do you do?" Now I was kind of curious.

"My dance group is a semi-finalist on American Idol." He sounded very humble and sincere.

The way he said it suddenly arose sympathy in me towards the stranger who put both of us in this awkward situation. The smell did not feel that bad anymore. Finally, we started driving towards our destination. He was telling me about his auditioning and dance group he was part of, his difficult childhood, and plans for future.

"Great," I thought, feeling satisfied, "I am glad that the situation is under control and we are heading to where we need to go!"

"Can I please use your aux cord to play my music?" Andre asked very politely as always. "I want to get into my auditioning mood."

"Sure." I answered and gave him the loose end of the cord. I had no idea of what kind of music we are going to listen to and what will be going through my mind.

His choice of music started out with some rhythmic hip-hop song featured by a known rap artist. It was easy to listen to, so I assumed it to be a perfect dance song, even more, because my passenger was a professional dancer.

"Cool." I thought and for a moment enjoyed the sound produced by a powerful Harman Kardon sound system installed in my truck. I love good music and my passenger's choice was not bad at all!

"Can you please turn the volume up?" Andre asked his usual way. This guy really knew how to get what he wanted as it was impossible to say "no" to him.

"Of course!" I said and turned the volume up.

"More please." He sounded serious and determined.

I did what he asked. Then he asked a few more times. I was curious at what volume he would finally stop asking, so I followed his requests until he said, "Thank you, that's good." The way volume goes in my truck, the comfortable sound is at level 7, but we were listening to his rap at sound level 21.

"Fantastic!" I thought and for a moment imagined as if I was doing this alone. "I am driving in my truck, all four windows down (for a known reason) and blasting rap songs. Good that I am far from home where no one knows me..." I was not able to hide the smile that was stretching the corners of my lips from one ear to another. "What are you doing, lady?" I continued the inner dialogue while smiling on the outside, "It is so not you!"

He changed the songs, some skipping, some fast-forwarding until he found the exact one, he wanted to listen to. We stopped at the red light next to two other cars. Windows down, music blasting.

"Wasted, I'm on these drugs, I feel wasted

...

Wasted, I waste all my time when I'm wasted

...

She do cocaine in my basement"*

These lines of the lyrics were still pulsating in my brain long after I let my passenger out. THAT was one of the most embarrassing moments I have ever experienced. I could look neither left nor right standing at the red light, although I could sense quite a few surprised faces staring in my direction, trying to find some sense in what was happening.

(*Wasted by Juice WRLD)

It was the most real (and surreal at the same time) experience of "walking in someone else's shoes." And I am glad that I let it happen, because when and how I would ever know how it feels? The way it all started and continued, I wanted to get a full spectrum of emotions generated by living life Andre's style. Also, it was a good way to test my limits that came close to being reached.

Well, we finally arrived.

"Thank you so much for the ride. You are awesome!" Andre said as always politely and asked if he could give me a hug.

A HUG it was, and he left.

The chances that we would see each other again are close to zero, but there is something that will live on—a little seed of goodness that was planted uniting our differences, eliminating judgment, and caring to understand.

Our first instinct is to judge something or someone that does not meet our expectations or is different in any way. We really must make an effort to listen, observe and to start understanding each other.

We must open our minds and hearts to make this world a better place!

Chapter 6.

"No Returning Customers..."

"It is not joy that makes us grateful.
It is gratitude that makes us joyful."

~ David Steindl-Rast ~

J ust another fresh start of the day, sunny Monday morning in Chicago, which is one of the most beautiful cities in the world. 2.7 million people call this beautiful city their home. It makes Chicago the third largest city in the US. New York with 8.5 million is in the first place and Los Angeles with 3.9 million is in second place.

Chicago is famous for its unique architecture and for having one of the world's tallest and most magnificent city skylines. It is a very friendly, clean, and welcoming city. Chicago has its own Chicago style hot dogs and deep-dish pizza.

All the above and the fact that Chicago is also a business mecca, Chicago International Airport (O'Hare) was the nation's busiest airport in 2018 in terms of total flights. The total number of flights in and out of O'Hare was 900,000, handling a total of 83 million passengers. On the busiest day, there were close to 3000 arrivals and departures.*

Back to the beautiful morning. I was driving to O'Hare airport to pick up my first passenger of the day. All I knew about him was his name—Brad. I was driving to pick up Brad and trying to guess where he could possibly be going. As it was 8:00 a.m. on Monday, my guess was downtown Chicago. This was the time when people arrive for business and their destination, for the most part, was the city.

There was my Brad, waving "Hello," apparently recognizing the truck as it was what the app said. I was close to guessing Brad's destination; he was going to one of the Chicago breweries located in Old Town, which is a neighborhood North of downtown.

"Good morning!" said Brad.

"Good morning!" I answered, as we slowly started moving.

*(*Source:Chicago Tribune, February 4, 2019).*

"Do you drink beer?" Brad surprised me with the question. He took me aback because first, it was too early in the morning to think about alcohol, secondly because I do not drink at all. I did not want to disappoint him but could not lie either.

"No." I said, "The only occasion I would use beer is to rinse my hair!"

"Hair?" Brad asked in complete disbelief thinking that I was joking or making fun of him.

"Yes, hair! It is a hairstyling trick that my grandma taught me."

"Hmmm... for real?" Brad was still doubting my truthfulness as he had never heard anyone telling him anything like this.

"Didn't mean to start a hairstyling conversation with you but yes, beer holds the hairstyle perfectly!" I confirmed that I meant what I said.

"Interesting..." Brad said, extending a pause before continuing. "I will tell my mom. She is a hairdresser."

"Absolutely! Not sure if she can use this method on her customers though. Beer is alcohol, so she might be required to apply for an alcohol license." I said and we both laughed at the idea of his mom being a beautician with an alcohol license.

As we continued to develop the subject and laughed, Brad said something that changed the direction of my thoughts from being funny to totally confused. "The only problem—my mom will never know if the beer worked. She does not have returning customers."

"No returning customers?" Now I asked in disbelief thinking how bad of a hairdresser Brad's mom was. But then I thought even if she were THAT bad, people would come back to at least complain.

"No returning customers because she works at a funeral home and all her customers are deceased." Brad cleared up my confusion by making everything even more confusing.

This was one of the most awkward moments I had experienced in my Rideshare history. The moment of silence that followed Brad's last sentence felt like an eternity. The amount and the size of the thoughts running through my mind seemed to be too big to fit the outlet of the processed information. It took quite a while for me to respond, as I did not know if I should apologize for starting the subject or it was still as funny as when we were laughing.

"Yeah, I have to lie down when she does my hair, as this is the only position she knows how to cut hair," he said and started laughing louder than before.

Oh my God, was this for real? Did I just hear that? This guy had a pretty harsh sense of humor. Well... yeah... um... aaaaaaa...

Brad continued laughing at his own joke as he saw how lost I was trying to come up with anything to say.

"That's pretty unusual." I mumbled trying to balance the respect I had for his mom for doing what she was doing (just think about it, somebody must do it!), and the urge to laugh along with the man sitting in my truck laughing out loud.

"How did she get into doing something like that?" I asked when we took a break from laughing.

"I guess it was one of those meant to be things for my mom," said Brad. "She has been doing it her whole life. I have no idea how she got her first 'customer' though... Hope, no one died in her chair." Brad kept his bold sense of humor unleashed.

The ride was over. "Have a great week!" Brad said, getting out of the truck.

"Thank you! You, as well—have a great week!" I said before he closed the door.

That was quite an awakening start of the day, just another time making me think—how many people out there do things we have no idea exist. We simply do not think about all the unusual, irregular, specific jobs, and things some people have to do. Grateful for all of them as they make it easy for everybody else who needs their services.

Chapter 7.

"I Just Walked the Walk of Shame"

"You can never tell a book by its cover."

~ Edwin Rolfe ~

I t was around 8:00 a.m. on a beautiful sunny Saturday morning in downtown Chicago. As I was waiting for my first passenger, I noticed a person coming out from the apartment building dressed as a woman, walking like a man. The person looked to the right, then to the left, then on her phone. Was that my Tiffan(y)? I guess so because next she came straight to my truck.

"I just walked the walk of shame," was the first thing she said when she opened the back door of my truck. Yes, even before "Good Morning."

"Well, tell me about it! What's your shame?" I questioned, going along with the conversation she so eagerly started.

"I can't believe I got involved with him. So disgusting." She went on and on and on describing the man, how they met, and the reasons why she ended up in his place.

She kept mentioning the "Walk of Shame" because the man had weird requests that she could not fulfill so she had to leave early.

With all my curiosity, I did not want to know what kind of requests and what kind of man...

I had never seen so many "add-ons" on one person. Hair, eyelashes, lips, cheeks, chin, breasts, butt, nails. That is all I could see, who knows what else there was.

Honestly, I still do not know if that was a woman or a man, I am leaning towards a man, though. In the end, it did not really matter. Tiffany identified as female and it was fine with me. As soon as she got over the shame part, she turned out to be such an interesting person.

When we arrived at Tiffany's destination, she felt a lot better because she had gotten everything that was bothering her off her chest. She asked if she could shake my hand.

"Sure," I said, reaching out to her.

She took my hand with both of her hands and said one of the most sincere thank you I have ever heard. Then she left, taking a little part of me with her.

P.S. You might have seen her, as she works in one of the big department stores on Michigan Avenue in Chicago. Just in case you do see her, tell her that I said "Hello!"

Sometimes, something that seems so obvious turns out to be completely something else. We are quick to judge just because someone looks different, has different taste and attitude towards life. However, this person has feelings the same way you do. This person wants to be loved, respected, and accepted. We all are trying to find our place in this world to fit in and be happy.

Someone like Tiffany is one of the bravest people I have ever met. She is going against the flow, against normal (what is normal?) and against stereotypes. I would like to wish her good luck in finding herself and be in peace with who she is.

Chapter 8.

"F***ing Slowpokes!"

"I destroy my enemies when I make them my friends."

~ Abraham Lincoln ~

J ust another busy Friday afternoon. Traffic was heavy as usual. Everybody was "happily" commuting to start enjoying their weekend.

I picked up a guy in one of the wealthiest Chicago suburbs. When you think "wealthy," you by default also consider that it is safe.

Well...

Here is how it all went. On a quick note before I continue—this was the only passenger in my two-year Rideshare career who I reported to Rideshare. The only passenger who I did not rate because I simply turned off the app. I did not want any connection with this person.

It was 3:00 p.m. when I arrived at his gated property. When I accepted the ride, I could see that the ride was going to be fifty-four minutes long. He came out with a pile of papers in his left hand and the phone in his right.

Let's call him David.

David got into the truck, and without replying to my greeting he abruptly asked about the traffic. I told him that the ride was going to be close to an hour. He surprised me with what he said: "Bullsh*t. It normally takes no more than thirty minutes."

I looked at him in disbelief, as I did not know how to react to such a statement. "Should I go, or should I not go? Do you want to cancel the ride?" I asked him, really hoping that he would get out. It just did not feel right from the very beginning.

"No. Start moving. I will see how that goes. I don't believe it is going to take an hour."

I started driving.

As soon as we got onto the highway, he started commenting on the cars to his right and in front of us. He was calling the drivers names saying that they did not know how to drive and that was the reason why HE needed to sit in the traffic.

"F***ing slowpokes!" Suddenly he yelled so loud that I hit the brakes. "Sorry," he said as quietly as possible when he saw what his reaction had caused me to do. "Sorry, OK?" He said it one more time, emphasizing "OK," as if he was running out of patience. He just wanted to make sure that I had accepted his "apology."

Usually, when someone's behavior is misleading, I ask questions. Simple questions. As such, by their answers I could better understand their intentions.

"Are you running late?" I asked him.

"Yes."

"Is it a date? Important meeting?" I tried to dig deeper to "disarm" him.

"No." David answered as dry and short as he could.

Fine, I thought to myself. Only thirty-five more minutes left for us to share this space and I would never see him again.

I kept driving; he kept commenting on the environment.

I was driving, thinking about my passenger in the backseat feeling confused, worried, and annoyed all at the same time. Suddenly, I sensed strange movements in the back. Do you know how sometimes you see something with the very corner of your eye, but it doesn't completely register at first?

David was banging his head against the headrest of the front seat. Wait, did I see it right? My cheeks turned red as the blood flow increased the speed.

He would do it for a while then he would "take a break." The next thing I heard was a clapping sound which turned out to be him slapping his cheeks. He went for a while with slapping. Then he tried to combine the headbanging with the cheek slapping but that did not work out as I assumed, he could not manage the synchronicity.

"What a talented guy!" I thought. "He must be a musician or otherwise connected with performing arts."

No, those were not my real thoughts. They were random sarcastic thoughts "supporting" this guy's obvious mental issues.

My heart was racing, my cheeks were burning, and my palms were wet.

"What a freak! What is he up to? Am I safe with him?" I could barely concentrate on the road.

His phone rang. "Hi daddy!" he answered in a sweet tone of his voice as if he were five years old. Apparently, it was his dad who was checking on him. Their conversation did not last long; David ended it with an abrupt "bye."

I cannot even guess what made him do what he did next. He played the anthem of the United States aloud on his phone and sang along. While singing he was also slapping his cheeks. Once he was done singing the anthem, he found a shooting video which he was watching and rewinding and watching again and again and again. There were screaming voices at first and then a sound of a long gunfire. There was a lot of suffering and pain in

those sounds that he was repeatedly listening to. He slowly leaned forward hitting the headrest with his forehead then sitting straight, then forward, straight... again and again and again.

Mentally, this was the longest ride I have ever given to anybody. I was thinking about stopping and letting him out but that did not feel like a good idea at the time, as I did not know what this person was capable of. What gave me hope was that at some point he complimented me on saving some time by "tricking the traffic." I drove in the airport exit lane for a while and then got back in the lane where the mainstream of the cars was. It really saved us good ten minutes. I was surprised that he saw that despite all his performing activities.

As soon as this ride was over, I called Rideshare support and reported this passenger. I really hope that no other driver will ever have to go through what I went through.

There was really nothing I wanted to take from this ride. I tried to connect with David to better understand the motives behind his weird movements and actions. He did not allow, and we did not become "friends."

Although nothing he did was targeted towards me directly, the level of discomfort he created in me was unbearable. All I wanted was to lose HIM on the way.

Do not judge the book by its cover! If the book is expensive does not always mean that the content is valuable. It can turn out to be the worst book you have ever read.

Still, I wish him well and hope that the roads he needs to take are traffic-free.

Chapter 9.

"Do You Want To Take My Seat?"

"How we perceive a situation and how we react to it is the basis of our stress. If you focus on the negative in any situation, you can expect high stress levels. However, if you try and see the good in the situation, your stress levels will greatly diminish."

~ Catherine Pulsifer ~

I picked up Sally at the airport. By her appearance and body language, I could tell that she was a (self-proclaimed) VIP—a skirt suit, high heels, a stylish computer purse in one hand, and a phone in the other.

The first thing she asked was the estimated arrival time. By the tone of her voice, I could sense how the whole world was slowly spinning around her, for her, and because of her. For this reason, I was not surprised when she was not hiding her disappointment by throwing a little tantrum learning about the traffic on our way.

"Please, hurry up. I am running late for a very important meeting!" She said anyway, despite seeing a long red line in the GPS app clearly indicating that "hurrying up" was not an option.

Sally was on the phone the whole ride. She was trying to coordinate her presentation with the people in her office. Sounded as if she was reading it for the first time, not liking the wording, the charts, the length, and at some point, she had doubts if the format was even right.

My passenger was late, not prepared, stressed out, and angry.

I could hear Sally throwing the sheets of paper all over the place, hissing, breathing loudly, and completely losing control over her emotions.

She scared me when suddenly I heard a loud "Calm down!" She most likely muted her phone so that the person on the other end did not hear her moment of weakness.

The traffic was not helping, we were moving with a speed of five miles per hour. I could feel that Sally had built up her frustration to the point that she was ready to explode.

Can you imagine being trapped with someone like Sally in a small space? In addition, you are the one adding to her frustration because you are not moving fast enough.

"Can you take a different lane?" Somewhere in the background of flying papers and my passenger's loud breathing, I thought I heard something addressed to me.

I turned my head to the right looking for a confirmation that she was talking to me.

"Yes, I am talking to you. Can you take a different lane because this one is not moving?" She made it clear that I was not meeting her expectations. Before telling me that, she apologized to whoever was on the phone by saying that this traffic was ridiculous, and that she needed to give directions to her driver.

Enough was enough. To get me out of my peaceful balance, you must be the master of disrespectfulness.

"Most likely because you are so busy doing business, you haven't noticed that the lane next to us is not moving either. None of the lanes." The tone of my voice was firm enough to make it clear that I was not someone she could control or show her frustration to. To put her even more in her place I made an offer, "Do you want to take my seat? Maybe you can drive us faster?"

For the first time during the entire ride, there was silence. She was not ready to hear what she heard. I guess the effect was like getting a splash of cold water thrown into her face.

From here, I was ready that she could take it any possible way. And honestly, I could not have cared any less. If she wanted to pick a fight, I was ready.

To my surprise, this was what happened next.

"I got to go, can't talk anymore", she said into the phone, sounding suspiciously calm. I assume the person on the phone wished her good luck as she said, "Thank you," before hanging up the phone.

"I am so sorry... It is not your fault and I did not mean to be rude. I am just so stressed out because of the whole situation. This meeting is so important to me, but I am not prepared, and I am so late... I am losing my mind over it." I could hear she was barely keeping herself from crying.

Then, we had a short conversation about giving up on the need to control everything and everybody.

"The stress that you have built up inside—is it going to change the outcome of your meeting?" I asked Sally.

"No..." she answered so quietly that I could barely hear it. *A long sigh that followed the answer was a lot louder than the answer itself.* It clearly confirmed how exhausted she was, ready to release the despair that was bottled up inside eating her alive.

I was surprised how easily Sally gave up and how calm she became. All of a sudden, she turned into a completely different person.

Now we could discuss how her vision of the outcome and positive thoughts could make a difference in how she felt, how she performed and what impression she would leave. *Sally was open to whatever outcome there was going to be as she realized how light and easy it felt trusting all the obstacles instead of fighting them and trying to control.*

She accepted the idea that she would arrive right on time—the time she was supposed to be there, even if it were late.

At the end of the ride, she was calm, appreciative, and at ease that her meeting would go as well as it could.

"Thank you!" Sally said, emphasizing each word and left. Later, I saw a very generous tip with a note in the app: "You have no idea how well it went! Thank you for your patience in putting up with my madness and for your wisdom making it easy for me. THANK YOU."

I really did not expect such an outcome from the trip that started out the way it did. All is good that ends well, right? I am glad she was able to change her perspective about the situation that she had no control over other than having a positive attitude and allowing everything unfold according to the best of her intentions and abilities.

Chapter 10.

"Hurry Up, I Am in Pain!"

*"Don't ask the question if you don't want
to hear the answer."*

~ Edward Hegarty ~

W ish I could say that this was just another beautiful sunny morning in Chicago. It started out like that until I accepted my first ride, which was a shared pool ride. There was one passenger already in the back seat when my phone rang. I could see that the caller was related to the ride, so I answered the phone on a speaker.

"Where are you? What is taking you so long?" A loud woman's voice sounded desperate on the other end.

"Well... I just picked up my first passenger and now I am on my way to pick you up," I answered as professionally as I could.

"Hurry up, I am in pain!" She yelled and hung up the phone.

We were stopped at the red light when this conversation took place. I looked back at the guy who was in the back seat. He shrugged his shoulders in confusion confirming that he also heard what I heard.

You cannot measure the amount of stress a call like that puts on a driver. It is as if you take on the responsibility of unknown circumstances, just because someone counts on you. Someone you do not know, have never seen, but by the tone of their voice you are made to believe that their life depends on you.

We were approaching the address where the desperate caller needed to be picked up. Both of us could not believe what we saw.

A very pregnant woman was waving and walking to our direction. When I said, "very pregnant," I meant that she looked big and ready to have the baby at any minute.

Seeing that and remembering the call, *the only concern lingering on my mind was that I am not trained to deliver babies.* Neither was the other passenger in the back seat. All that poor guy could say was "I cannot believe this!"

71

"Should I suggest her to call an ambulance?" I asked the guy in the back.

Before he could answer, the woman opened the front passenger door and pulled herself in confirming that she knew what she was doing.

"Hurry up, take me to the hospital!" She demanded, almost breathless. You could tell that she was in a lot of pain...

Remember, this was a pool ride? There was another passenger waiting to be picked up and the guy in the back seat would be the first one to get out.

What would you do if you were me?

"Let's just go to the hospital," the guy in the back seat said forcefully. "Please! Hurry up!" For a second, I thought that they were related.

I asked her which hospital she needed to go to, found the address on Google Maps, and started driving. I could not use the Rideshare map because it was not her turn and it did not show the address where she needed to be dropped off.

The next ten minutes were spent listening to the pregnant passenger's moaning and groaning. *Ten minutes that felt like an eternity, only hoping that she was not going into labor just yet.*

We dropped her off at the emergency entrance of the hospital. Someone came out to greet her and took her from there.

Me and the guy in the back looked at each other. In silence. I could see a tremendous relief in his eyes, and I was sure he could see the same in mine.

Why was she alone in such a condition? Why was she using Rideshare, and not an ambulance? And to make it worse—a pool Rideshare, shared with other passengers?

These were the questions going through my mind the whole time she was in my car. I never asked them because I did not want to know the answers. I felt like whatever her answer could be it would only create more questions.

Anyways, let's look at the bright side. If she delivered the baby that day, he or she is about to turn one. Happy Birthday, Baby!

Chapter 11.

"Do You Know
Where You Are Driving?"

*"Panic causes tunnel vision.
Calm acceptance of danger allows us to more easily
assess the situation and see the options."*

~ Simon Sinek ~

This happened on a busy Friday afternoon when everybody was trying to leave the city to enjoy their long Labor Day weekend. The story requires a little geographical insight about Chicago to better understand the drama that took place in my truck.

Different sources provide different information but when you type the "size of Chicago" in a Google search. The first fact you get is that the size of Chicago is 234 square miles. Wikipedia confirms a very similar size which is 228 square miles. Without a doubt, Chicago is a very big city and per Wikipedia and other official sources, it is the third biggest city in the US by population.

In the late 1920s, sociologists at the University of Chicago subdivided the city into 77 distinct community areas to provide a better living. Those community areas later subdivided into over 200 informally defined neighborhoods. The neighborhood names and identities have evolved over time due to real estate development and changing demographics.

Therefore, as you have learned—although the city is a singular governmental entity, it consists of many different areas that local people classify, categorize, and recognize based on what they hear on the news and what their family and friends say.

Long story short—there are popular neighborhoods, there are good, not so good, and bad neighborhoods. Guess what, there is one more category of neighborhoods in Chicago that you hear on national news (not just local news). Can we call them popular because of that? Maybe... but let's find out in what way.

On a quick note—no matter the statistics and information spread by news channels, there are people who live there and call it their home. They deal with the obstacles and hope for better. They accept all the good changes offered and implemented this way making small steps towards improvement.

Alright! The story can finally begin!

That Friday afternoon I was taken down South to Hyde Park, one of the neighborhoods that they say is developing and getting better. Whatever that means, I do not like to drive there and would normally set my destination back to the city. When I say, "the city," I mean the center of Chicago, downtown.

By the way, Hyde Park is home to the University of Chicago, the Museum of Science and Industry, and two of Chicago's four historic sites listed in the original 1966 National Register of Historic Places. Those two in Hyde Park are Chicago Pile-1, the world's first artificial nuclear reactor, and Robie House, a National Historic Landmark designed as a single-family home by famous architect Frank Lloyd Wright. In the early twenty-first century, Hyde Park received national attention for its association with the US President Barack Obama, who was a law lecturer at the University of Chicago, before running for president and used to live in Hyde Park with his family.*

I was not quick enough to set the destination in the Rideshare app back to the city before I was offered another ride that I saw was twenty-five minutes long. I accepted it and went to pick up Suzan from The University of Chicago Booth School of Business.

---

*(*Source: https://en.wikipedia.org/wiki/Hyde_Park,_Chicago)*

It was 5:00 p.m., and the area felt empty as everybody had left already. Suzan was standing outside by herself, holding the handle of a big suitcase by her side. No doubt, she was going to an airport.

As soon as Suzan got into my truck, her body language and a dry "hello" made it clear that she did not want to communicate because she was either very tired, annoyed, or simply an antisocial individual. All the above was fine with me.

Her destination was the airport. With all the busy roads, I had to figure out which route to take. The fastest route was a straight line (seven and a half miles) taking streets and going through the neighborhoods or we could spend thirty-five minutes extra and take two highways (fifteen miles). Sometimes I would ask my passengers which route they would prefer but this time it looked so obvious that I did not bother Suzan with my question. Plus, she did not seem to care about anything but her phone which she was excessively using as I could hear a continuous typing sound.

We started driving towards the airport taking the streets. Little did I know what streets and what neighborhoods our route included... As soon as we left the University of Chicago territory, strange scenes started to appear. Empty streets with garbage dumped left and right. Abandoned houses without windows as they were covered with plywood sheets. I was driving and thinking to myself, "Good that Suzan doesn't care and is busy enough not to look around." I could see in the rearview mirror that her eyes were constantly on her phone.

Honestly, as positive and optimistic as I am, that neighborhood really creeped me out. There were very few people on the streets who only added to the thriller-like atmosphere. They would cross the street wherever and whenever they pleased without paying attention to the cars passing by. *The only assurance that everything was going to be alright came from the police cars roaming around on every corner looking like sharks and hunters at the same time.*

I did not know which neighborhood we were driving through when suddenly there was a big advertisement on the wall. It was quite worn out and pale, but I could still read what it said. Englewood Auto Care. The business was closed, and the building was demolished but at least I knew where we were. I had never been there before, and had only heard people say that Englewood is one of the most impoverished neighborhoods in Chicago.

"Do you know where you are driving?" For the first time, I heard Suzan talking. The sound of her voice interrupted my thought process and emotional survival mode. The question came suddenly but at the same time, it was long overdue as she was inquiring about the area that we had been driving through for a while.

"Yes, I am taking you to the airport," I replied as calmly as I could.

"No, I meant the area where we are at—do you know where we are?" She continued asking questions.

Good that I just read the advertisement on the wall, so I could tell her the exact location *(which I would have never told her if I knew what her reaction was going to be)*. In addition, it felt as if she knew where we were, and she was just testing me and trying to pick a fight.

"Englewood." My answer was short and dry.

"Englewood consistently ranks as one of the most dangerous neighborhoods in the city. For those who do not live there and are unlikely to ever visit, WGN offers you a glimpse of life on the streets. In just twelve hours, we witnessed more trouble than most will see in their lifetime." [1]

"It's Englewood. That is a refrain we would hear over and over. It is Englewood as if that explains all that is wrong in this part of town. It's the kind of place where something as simple as a dice game could turn deadly because a group of men are hanging out." [2]

"Englewood in Chicago is a neighborhood that lives up to its reputation. It has a high crime rate, lots of boarded-up houses, and is generally not a place you want to be at night." [3]

Because of this ride, I did a research about Englewood. I could go on and on citing different internet sources describing how bad Englewood was. *Just reading all that gave me enough information to mark this territory as the one to avoid.* DO NOT ENTER would have to be the sign from all sides of this neighborhood.

But then again—people live there having hopes for a better life, better schools, and future for their children.

I was driving and thinking: "How could it historically develop into a neighborhood it was and why did it have to live up to its reputation for so long?" *No news channel gives you an answer or a solution. They only add to the drama creating negative emotions*

([1,2,3] Source: various internet sites).

and making everybody believe that the place is dangerous and threatening.

I do not know if I could classify this as "on a positive note" but NBA player Derrick Rose and American Idol finalist and Oscar winner Jennifer Hudson both were born and raised in Englewood neighborhood. If you do not know what happened to Jennifer's family, there are many online sources where you can find a complete story of her tragedy.

Suzan started breathing so fast and loud that for a second, she could not talk.

"Englewood?" She finally spat the word out in a form of a question. "Do you drive here often? Do you know what neighborhood this is? Where are all the people? OMG, did you see that house? And who is that person on the corner?" Suzan would not stop asking questions that clearly indicated that she was in a state of panic.

"Suzan, do I look like I belong here? Exactly, I do not belong here, so I do not normally drive here. The matter of fact, in my two years of driving for Rideshare, this is the first time I am taking this route. Please, do not panic, we are almost through this neighborhood. Only twelve minutes are left until we will arrive at the airport. Let's think positive thoughts! Plus, we are driving in a pickup truck, which is big, high, and fast!"

I believe in the Law of Attraction when we attract things or events that we think about or want the most. Unfortunately, we attract the things we do not want or are afraid of as well. As long as we give something enough energy by thinking about it, we activate the Law. This is the reason why my thoughts are positive even in the worst possible situations. I am looking for a positive outcome no matter what.

She was cutting close to her boarding time, so she took a deep breath and said, "Yes, you are right. Let's think positively."

There was a police car next to us that pretty much escorted us all the way to the end of the bad part of the city. Both of us silently released the tension.

Normally I would say that we are put in a certain situation for a reason. In this case, I am still wondering if it happened because of me or because of Suzan. Or both? For some reason, Suzan had to get into my truck and experience what she experienced. At the end of the ride, she was extremely nice and talkative, and she apologized for being rude.

These were the longest and the most tiring three miles I have ever driven.

All is good that ends well. Lesson learned. I would definitely spend extra thirty minutes and drive seven miles more to avoid everything that was written above.

I am grateful for every situation I have been put through, grateful for every positive outcome, every lesson learned. Thankful for every person I have met on my way, as we are each other's best teachers.

Chapter 12.

"Just Come and Get Her Out of My Way"

"Life is an echo. What you send out, comes back.
What you sow, you reap. What you give, you get.
What you see in others, exists in you.
Remember, life is an echo.
It always gets back to you. So give goodness."

~ Chinese Proverb ~

I am going to tell you something that I am not proud of. But it did happen. I suffered, and most importantly, I learned. A LOT. I was debating whether I should include this in the book or not because it is so out of my character. I decided to include it because anybody could end up in my place and hopefully, my experience would serve as an example of how to stop the situation before it would go out of control.

Just a few hours ago in the morning, I was writing the previous chapter about Englewood. I did a lot of reading and researching about the area I was writing about. I could feel how negativity was taking over my mood and left me feeling anxious, annoyed, and weighed down.

So, I left the house in this condition. It did not start smoothly, and it did not go smoothly...

I decided to go to the airport and from there go with the flow, meaning—I had no other plan than to go into the direction my passenger needed to go. Because of a poor cellular reception at the airport I could not accept any ride, that is why after spending fifty-five minutes waiting for a ride, I ended up driving away by myself. It was nothing new just a little more annoying than usual because of my already ruined mood.

Fast forward. I ended up driving to the city where I got my first ride of the day. A cute French couple going to the Museum of Science and Industry. Maybe you remember from the previous chapter that the museum was in Hyde Park...

This ride was nothing special, small talk about the weather in Chicago and them being excited to explore the city. I stopped at the museum entrance, let my French passengers out, and was about to leave. I just needed to figure out where to go from there.

What happened next is a proof of how quickly everything can change. No one else is in charge of what you are experiencing but

87

*you. The explanation is very simple—you are inviting into your life
EVERYTHING that is happening to you. It can be a good change
or as in this situation—not so good.*

While I was trying to figure out which way I should be going,
somewhere in the background I heard a honking sound with every
single beep getting longer and louder. At first, I was not paying full
attention to what was happening around me because I was busy
searching the map on my phone.

The sound would not stop. Subsequently, I looked up; in front
of me was a taxicab. I looked in the rearview mirror and there was
another taxicab behind me.

"Wait a second!" Suddenly it dawned on me: "Is he honking at
me?"

While it took me a moment to register the situation, the cab behind drove and stopped next to me.

I rolled down the window as I could see that the driver was
about to say something to me. *With all my naivety, I thought that
something had happened, and he needed help.*

What happened next really blew my mind. He yelled at me that
I was in a taxi line and needed to leave or he was going to call the
police and report me.

I could not believe what I had just heard. Seriously, man? The
time I spent searching the map after I let my previous passengers
out was one minute at most. The taxi in front of me did not move
even an inch. Clearly, there was no way I was holding up the taxi
line.

It blew my mind, and it also blew my senses out of balance.

"Are you in a hurry?" I asked the taxi driver after he finished the sentence with the threat of reporting me. My voice was quiet, the intonation was calm. Maybe I stretched the words a little bit longer than a fluent speaker would require. That and the fact that one corner of my mouth was smirking at him, gave out the sarcastic meaning of my question.

"You are in my spot," he kept yelling at me.

"I was about to leave but now I am not going to," I told him in the same calm manner. I do not remember experiencing such an audacity, especially, when there was no reason. I understand that taxi drivers are less busy because of Rideshare but he has an equal opportunity to drive for Rideshare as I do. There was no reason to be rude to me because I was not planning on staying and taking away his passengers.

"I am calling the police; they will come and give you a ticket," he said, shaking his little fists at me.

"Please do so. Call whomever you need to call!" I was going with the plot of his nonsense because I wanted to know how far he was ready to go with it.

He grabbed his phone and showed a huge effort by pressing each button on his phone, dialed the number. Then he enthusiastically walked to the front of my truck and started dictating the license plate number. Oh, I completely forgot to mention, before calling anyone, we had a little "photo shoot." He was taking pictures of the

truck's license plate in the front and back, and the pictures of your one and only—me! For a moment, I felt like a celebrity and joked with him that I did not feel picture ready. However, on a serious note, this picture taking act made it all even more dramatic and obvious that he was serious about his intentions, threats, and actions.

I did not know if there was anybody listening to him when he called or if he was performing a one-man standup "comedy." It honestly was very clumsy and not funny at all.

"Just come and get her out of my way." He said it at least three times on the phone. When he was done talking on the phone, he confirmed with me that THEY are on the way.

"Who are THEY?" I asked him.

"The cops." He sounded very proud of himself.

"Great! They will see the obvious—you have blocked my way and I can't get out." Now I could barely hold my laugh. It was true—when he stopped next to me, there was no way I could get out of there. He jumped back in his car and backed up a little.

"So, you are not afraid?" He could not hide his false excitement of a "victory."

"No, I am not. Because I have not done anything wrong." While I said that, I was given my next passenger in the Rideshare's app. The pickup location was a few yards down, by another museum entrance.

I wished the taxi driver a wonderful day and slowly started driving. He jumped out of his car and ran to my side window to mock me: "Oh, I am not afraid. Then why are you leaving if you are not afraid?"

"I was just given a ride, sorry, have to go. It was nice meeting you. Have a good life." My patience started to wear out as he was really getting on my nerves.

"Oh really? Then you are not leaving!" He walked to the front of the truck and blocked my way with his body.

Well... What can I say...

Thankfully, there was so much attention to the taxi driver's antics from the other drivers and the passing museum visitors that my new passionate friend decided to give up.

Thus, we both gave up on each other and parted ways.

This was one of these unexplainable situations—how in the world I could get myself into something like this? Why did I have to play along?

Apparently, I had to as I was attracting it all with my own energy that was soaked with negativity since my early morning research time. We both were on the same frequency with the taxi driver who was raiding the streets looking for his next prey.

This was the culmination of the day. It did not get any more intense after that but "cooling off" had a pattern that was not coincidental. Let me show you how it unfolded.

My next two passengers were two really nice guys from Spain who I was taking to a helicopter ride. I usually do not complain or comment on my passengers because there is enough time to cool off in between rides, even if something unusual would have happened on a previous ride. This pick-up location was so close that I came to pick them up still feeling HOT.

I did not go into details about the incident; I just said that the taxi driver was rude towards me. They told me about the fights taxi drivers had with Rideshare in Barcelona. As a result, there was no Rideshare in Barcelona for a while.

"Wish I could've told this to my new taxi buddy," I thought. "Maybe he should consider moving to Barcelona." I did not have to force my thoughts to be mean. They were overflowing on their own. Thank goodness, I never said it out loud. "Stop it, already!" I screamed at myself in my head. "It is about time to calm down and get over it!" I continued to convince myself as a part of a therapy in recovering from a recent drama.

I let these guys out and started driving to pick up my next passenger. I did not notice when I accepted the ride that it was a pool ride. To my surprise, quickly enough there was another passenger added and another.

I wanted to cancel that thread of the rides because the area was shady and based on my rules, which are not really rules but simple common sense, I had to go offline. I went against my own intuition and logically ended up where I was supposed to end up THAT day.

I went to pick up Jacob, a very talkative young man, who was going home from work. We were chatting all the way, until we picked up the two other passengers.

Jacob was the first one to be dropped off. As we were approaching his destination, the area looked awfully familiar. He got out, and I asked if anyone knew what area it was.

"Englewood," the girl next to me answered very firmly, the way there was no more discussion.

Who would want any discussion on Englewood anyway, right? The next ten minutes until I let the girl out, I had a profoundly serious "conversation" in my head. The way my day was going and the area I was taken back into AGAIN, made it a complete circle on the map. The circle that would hopefully put to an end the cycle of the above described day's negative events. Those events were accruing, one after another. *It felt like a slow-motion movie where I was shown and explained what reality I was creating for myself by allowing negativity and paying attention to unwanted things. No doubt—the Law of Attraction is REAL.*

As soon as the girl left, the guy in the back seat quietly asked if I really did not know what area that was. Honestly, I did not want to talk about it anymore, so I said. "No, I did not know."

He got out of my truck, and I turned off the app and drove as far away from that neighborhood as I could.

That was the last ride of that day. I got home leaving all the negativity outside and behind. DONE.

What a day...

No one is perfect. We all are a work in progress, all of us occasionally have "those days." The good news—we can actually learn how to have control over how we feel and what kind of days we are having. And then, even if we let ourselves "loose" on emotions, we can choose how deep we want to experience the things and events like I described above. The recipe is very simple—as soon as you notice an inner discomfort, check your thoughts. Like in my situation with the taxi driver. *My thoughts about the situation made it all so much worse.* Those were my thoughts that kept convincing me that he was rude, that the situation was unfair, and that I was wronged. A thousand other little thoughts came together in my mind where they all felt invited. The thoughts continued because I did not stop them. It would have made a big difference if I "blocked" my thoughts by changing their direction to feeling good thoughts.

Long story short—I am in charge of what I think. This also puts me in charge of how I feel about myself. The better I feel about myself, the better days I am having. The list of all the benefits of having good thoughts can be extended to better relationships and a better life in general. At the end of such a day I described above, the only thing I could do is to regret the emotions wasted. Even knowing how the Law of the Universe works, there are days like that. I guess we need them to refresh what we already know.

Let's be nice to each other. I have seen quite a few road rages; they do not lead anywhere, and they do not solve anything. Do you know what does? If someone is in a hurry and they want to cut you off, let them in because you never know what their emergency is. If there is none, you do not have to be the

one to decide and to judge. Instead of forcing the situation by "teaching the lesson," think about your safety, well-being, and peace of mind. Believe me—sooner or later they will have to learn their lesson, which will be taught in their own way.

If we are nice to each other, we see more smiles and hear more nice words. If someone is rude to you, break that spell by being genuinely nice to that person because they may need it the most. Even if it seems impossible at first, try, it makes such a big difference. Wishing the taxi driver all the best and hope that his days are filled with joy, and he stays busy taking his passengers where they need to go.

Chapter 13.

"Just in Case I Get Raped"

*"Exaggeration wastes distinction and testifies
to the paucity of your understanding and taste."*

~ Baltasar Gracian ~

The sound of pouring rain accompanied by thunder and lightning strikes in the background created a perfect Friday the 13th atmosphere. As a matter of fact, it was a Friday.

I picked up Kimberly by one of the high-rise office buildings in downtown Chicago. She had a suitcase by her side, which gave me a hint that she might be going to the airport.

Kimberly opened the back door of my truck, threw in her suitcase, and climbed in herself. She was soaked with water from the rain. It seemed like there was no dry spot on her.

"I hope you don't mind me putting my suitcase in here," she said when she got in.

"No, not at all!" I replied and started driving.

"I always have my bags with me when I use rideshare," she kept explaining herself.

"Sure." I had nothing else to say.

It was raining so heavily that the window wipers were working at full speed and I could still barely see through. I really had to put in an extra effort to concentrate on the road.

"It's just in case I get raped, you know?" Kimberly supported her justification.

Wait, what? I was not sure if through all that noise I heard it right.

"Raped?" I asked and al-most giggled.

"Yes, I just want to be pre-pared to jump out if I need to." Kimberly finished her justification.

Was she joking or was she drunk? She really seemed to

mean what she had just said, though. I guess, there was something that I did not know and honestly, did not want to know.

"You are safe with me!" I was trying to stay respectful while managing to get over her strange reasoning.

We drove in silence. I mean—we did not talk. The rain, the thunder, and the lightning kept playing their symphony making this Friday night the one to remember.

Let's leave this mystery unsolved, living in the darkness of the nightly sky with threatening thunder and pouring rain. Whatever was the reason behind Kimberly's statement it was not appealing enough to explore the truth behind it. A little detail that I would not normally mention but in this case, it might help to understand my confusion—Kimberly was a grown woman in her sixties. It made me wonder about her tendency to exaggerate things to the point that she would have to make sure that her woman driver knew that she was ready to jump out of the car if needed. Just the visual of that made me smile. Let's hope that Kimberly does not ever have to make that jump!

Chapter 14.

"It's Shooting Equipment"

*"Perception is a guess or estimate of what is 'out there'
depending on how we read the clues; therefore,
it can never be absolute and often is unreliable."*

~ Earl Kelley ~

J ust another rainy afternoon in Chicago. I was on my way to pick up a person by name of Suri from Eataly, one of the popular restaurants in Chicago. All I could see before I picked her up was that the ride was going to be forty-two minutes long. A woman wearing what I learned is a niqab (only the area around her eyes was clear) was waiting for me at the curbside of the restaurant. Suri was extremely talkative. As soon as she got into the truck, she laughed and said that she was completely soaked in the rain, but that she did not really mind because she was on THAT important mission.

"Great," I thought to myself, "we have a long ride and the passenger is open to talking, and I cannot wait to hear about her mission!"

Suri politely asked me if I did not mind making a quick stop on Michigan Avenue, where her friend was waiting for her and would be going with us.

"Sure!" I answered because I had never had any problem with my passengers asking to make a stop.

It was the entrance of a Hilton hotel on Michigan Avenue in the city. *I am not really supposed to be stopping or standing there but I thought a quick stop while the person jumped in the truck was OK.*

"There he is!" Suri said, opened the door and got out of the truck as soon as we stopped in front of the hotel. The only person I saw was an army-built tall man all covered in tattoos standing outside the hotel entrance. Next to him were three huge black plastic storage boxes and a case.

She rushed out to ask if he needed help to load all that in the truck.

OK... I don't know how to properly explain what was going through my mind seeing all that, but one thing was clear the feeling was not comfortable as these people certainly looked like they had nothing in common, totally incompatible, the biggest mismatch possible.

"Fine, let's put the judgment aside and go with the flow," I thought, trying to convince myself that I should not believe everything I think...

Apparently, he refused her help because she got right back into the back seat of the truck. I was not prepared for this long pitstop on the street where I was not supposed to stop for even a second (Note: *There is another entrance on the other side where normally all the pickups are made.*) I was instinctively looking in all possible directions making sure that there was no one running at us with a traffic ticket. Suri was apologizing that this was taking so long because she probably saw that I was getting nervous.

Suddenly the back door of the truck opened wide and the man holding the smallest black case appeared in it. He asked Suri very formally, "Do you want me to take this inside?"

"Yes, we might use it on the way," the way Suri answered, I could tell that she was the one in charge of whatever was happening.

The man left the case on the floor next to where he was going to sit. He went back outside to make sure that all the boxes were loaded and secured.

"Just curious what is in those boxes?" I asked Suri without any idea of what her answer might be.

"It's shooting equipment," she replied in ONE short sentence.

When she said it, she most definitely did not realize what an impact her answer had left on your one and only.

A complete brain freeze in seconds.

I do not know how long it took me to release the panic mode in my brain because it was not functioning for a while.

"Oh my God... Are you serious? I knew something was in the air!" I tried to stay calm as I was changing colors from pale to red (to be exact—dark RED). *My head was pulsating, my heart was racing, there was a red light blinking in front of my eyes and a whistling noise blowing in my ears. I could not breathe, could not move, and could not talk.*

"Should I jump out of the truck? Should I ask her to leave before he gets in? Should I act cool? Should I ask questions, or should I keep quiet? Should I call 911 or should I simply yell for help?"

"Helllllp," was the muted sound in my brain desperately looking for the relief from the tension.

"No, this cannot be happening to me... Why?" I continued my inner dialogue.

There were many people passing by, minding their own business. No one saw those huge boxes being loaded into my truck, no one knew about the little black case inside the truck. No one would notice if I got "voluntarily kidnapped" in the middle of the day driving away in my own pickup truck loaded with the shooting equipment along with two people going on THAT important mission.

I was too busy processing different plans of escape that I did not notice how the army man got into the truck. I ended up with no plan the moment he interrupted my thought process by saying, "We are ready to go."

It was a totally surreal feeling. On one hand, I was willingly agreeing to do something against my will, through fear and doubt. On the other hand, I did not want to appear as an overreacting and over-exaggerating driver who had watched one too many action movies and had all the wrong ideas.

Next, I guess I pressed the gas pedal. My foot was numb, so technically I could have hit anything with it because I did not feel the direction it was going. We started moving, so I assume that I did hit the right lever in order to start moving. My brain was not connecting; I was operating the vehicle without being present.

Reality check—a lady, a muscle-bound tattooed man holding a little black mystery case in the back seat, and a trunk loaded with shooting equipment.

What would you do if you were me?

"How is your day going?" the man asked in a friendly manner.

"Are you kidding me? Don't you know how my day is going? I am frozen in fear from you and the mission I have become a part of. Aaahhhhh," I wanted to scream!

Instead, I organized my words in two simple sentences, "Thank you for asking. So far I can't complain."

Either my answer was too boring or it satisfied his interest because he did not ask me any more questions.

He and Suri exchanged a few phrases about the strategy they were going to use. Then they discussed the scenario if there were going to be two people or the whole family.

"Get me out of here! What in the world is happening? I don't want to be a part of any of this."

Still, thirty-five minutes to go...

"Do you want to shoot now?" the man asked Suri in a thriller-like voice.

"Yes, why not, let's try," she answered in the same voice.

The man leaned down to take the case. He opened it and...

Do you want to hear what was happening with me while they had this short exchange of words making an agreement to shoot? Exactly—you don't want to hear any more of my fearful feelings created by my own misconception.

So... he opened the case and took out his... video camera!

He was a professional videographer, and the lady was a representative of her country, visiting Chicago to make a documentary about a family that survived a terror act in their country. It was a historically well-known act of violence that took the lives of many people. The family that my passengers were on the way to visit survived the terror and moved to Chicago as refugees many years ago.

Can you recall that pleasant sensation in your body when it gradually turns warm from being frozen? It is as if you can feel where the bloodstream starts to circulate again creating that intense wave of relief. It is so good to be alive again!

Alright! To tell you the truth—the muscles were not that big anymore and the tattoos were fewer than what I saw in the beginning, the voice was nothing thriller-like at all. Very pleasant, caring, and talented people.

They asked me if I was OK if they "shot" me too and if I appeared in the documentary. I could finally speak and say what I thought. Thus, I answered that I don't know her country's history and I stand very far away from politics because in general, I am a lover, not a fighter. For all the above reasons, I respectfully said "no."

They were fine with that.

During the rest of the ride, he was interviewing and videotaping Suri.

The ride was over. The last thirty minutes went by faster than the first ten minutes.

They got the equipment out. The videographer gave me his business card just in case I would ever need to "shoot" anything.

Well... I might!

Guys... Seriously. This is a perfect example of what we are capable of creating in our heads! The more we think the more we start believing in what we are thinking. Be careful what thoughts you give power to or you can get DESTROYED by your own thinking. It has nothing to do with other people. My passengers had no idea what I was going through. They had no clue what story I had created in my mind—for them and for myself.

Do you see how easily a judgment is being created?

The lesson for life—if you want to know something, ask. Do not just assume. If it is still not clear, ask more questions. No matter our differences (views, religion, beliefs, preferences, and so on), we are all built from the same material. We operate on the same fuel and long the same things. We want to be happy. We want to love and to be loved. Simple as that and let's leave it this way.

Peace.

Chapter 15.

"Do You Eat the Bread That You Sell?"

"It's not fair to ask of others what you are not willing to do yourself. Practice what you preach."

~ Eleanor Roosevelt ~

R osemont is known for being a business district that includes one of the biggest convention centers in the city. It is located right next to O'Hare International Airport and many companies have their offices there because of how convenient the location is with lots of hotels, restaurants, and entertainment venues including a nearby casino.

Picking up a passenger in Rosemont most of the times would mean talking about their business.

This Wednesday morning was not an exception.

I arrived to pick up Anthony around 7:30 a.m. at one of the hotels in Rosemont.

There was a man in running shorts heading straight to my truck. He opened the front passenger door and got in. If the passenger is brave enough to get into the front seat it usually means that they are ready to communicate.

"Good morning!" Anthony sounded determined and ready to start his day.

"Good morning!" As a morning person myself, I could not be happier that someone besides me is full of energy and ready to rock and roll.

The ride was about fifteen minutes long. Anthony had a specific taste for coffee, so I was taking him to a certain store and back to get his cup of coffee.

"I need a cup of my favorite coffee before I can work out," he confirmed his plans and the importance of the mission of getting the coffee he likes.

We started talking. He said that he is in town because of his company's biggest event of the year—an annual regional manager meeting.

"Oh, yea? Tell me about it. What do you do? Are you a regional manager?" I asked, genuinely interested in my passenger's success story.

I felt like Anthony was waiting for this question so that he could proudly confirm that he was the regional manager in a well-known nationally distributed bread company.

The next five minutes he was telling me how important his job was and how much the company depended on him as he was taking care of the biggest region in the country. He was in charge of all big grocery store accounts in almost one-third of the states.

Just do not think that my Anthony was spending his days running around going to local grocery stores. No. Anthony worked on a corporate level, making deals wearing a white shirt and sitting at his desk in the office with an ocean view. He had to travel too, but it was always nice to leave the office and visit his customers to seal just another deal.

Anthony was with his company for over twenty years, so he really knew the product well and had worked his way up to be where he was.

Anthony had so many people reporting to him, his days were super busy making sure everybody everywhere was enjoying the products my passenger cares SO MUCH about.

I could tell Anthony was an amazing salesperson because he did not have to look for words, they were flowing like a river... disappearing without a trace of any chance to know if what he was telling was the truth.

I could see how good my passenger felt about himself by sharing his story.

"That is awesome, Anthony. I can tell that you really like your job!" I added to the size of his pride and continued with, "If you don't mind me asking, do you eat the bread that you sell?"

...

At least a minute of silence went by; I even looked at my passenger if he heard my question.

Do you know the look on someone's face when their eyes are nervously going different directions as if they were just caught in "crime" and were trying to find an explanation to their actions?

Anthony finally got over the "shock" and started describing how good the bread was. How the company was following all FDA guidelines on preservation, shelf life rules, and packaging requirements. He told me the statistics and gave a full sales report for the previous month, how the sales numbers were up compared to even a year before.

For a second, I felt like I was his boss and he was trying his best to prove his worth.

"Did I answer your question?" Anthony asked, after he finished his "report."

"The silence BEFORE your answer answered for you!" I could not stop a smile on my face wanting to support my conviction.

"Yeah..." was all Anthony could get out. "No one, in all my years of experience, had gotten me as bad as you just did with a simple question. I have always had an answer ready for all possible questions. I was not ready for this one..."

Anthony felt as if he just came down to Earth from his throne up high in the sky.

"Thank you so much," he said, adding, "I feel like in those ten minutes I learned more than in twenty years of the active sales job."

I am not going to lie; his honesty was flattering, especially because it came from such a "big shot."

Without any judgment. Just a question. How can one lead his life passionately offering something he does not believe in? What are the quality and real value of the world he has created around him?

Chapter 16.

"And the Winner Is!"

"A person's name is the doorway into their world;
a person's name has the power to open a connection..."

~ Luke Davis ~

A person's name has far more power than we can readily imagine. It is like a tag growing with us and into us since the day we are born. Our parents come up and start using this tag first. They want to get our attention so that we start complying with their simple commands like "eat your dinner," "go to bed," and "be quiet." We grow up being completely aware that when someone calls us by our name, they are seeking our attention.

Every time driving to pick up someone you definitely pay attention to the person's name. In most cases, you can determine the gender. But, then again, someone by the name Courtney could as well appear to be a guy.

Once I was waiting for Julie...

The door opened and the first thing I saw was a hairy man's arm followed by a hairy leg and head with a full beard... I asked if he was Julie, he said yes!

After meeting Courtney, I should have stopped questioning anybody's identity. Because, when I asked the guy who is that nice person Courtney who called Rideshare for him and he said that it was him, I felt truly embarrassed. It was awkward enough for me to learn and not to repeat it again. Well... you would think! The other day I met Alison. Guess who? Guess what? Yeah... another guy testing my stereotype zone.

What defeated me completely and hopefully for good is when I met George.

Yes, you guessed it right—George was a girl. As she was getting into the truck she asked if I am waiting for George, I said yes. Once she was inside, I said hello and asked how her day was going. She answered something and then I asked (just to regret a few moments later) what her name was.

"George, my n a m e i s G e o r g e." The way she said this sounded like in a slow-motion movie where every sound she made was stretched to emphasize the annoyance of having to answer this question AGAIN.

"OMG..." my thoughts wanted to explode, "so sorry, George..."

Then there was a moment of silence when I was trying to come up with some kind of sympathetically apologetic "concept" to loosen the tension that was lingering in the air.

"Is there a story behind your name?" That was all I could come up at that moment.

"No. I guess my parents just had a creative approach naming me," George's answer was dry.

That was it. We did not talk for the rest of the ride. I could not even say my regular "Have a good day, George" at the end of the ride. I was simply not brave enough to say "George" aloud.

Anyway...

With hairy Julie, we had a long, over an hour ride, and had an interesting conversation. At the very end, he said, "By the way, I forgot to tell you. My name is David. Julie is my cousin who called Rideshare for me."

At that point, believe me—it did not matter anymore if he was Julie or David especially when the whole hour I was "treating" him as if he was Julie.

With the names like Courtney, Alison, and George, you clearly have a visual before you meet these individuals (even though I failed with these particular ones). Nevertheless, there are names that you cannot possibly guess if that person is a man or a woman, although you can still pronounce the name. For example, Hui. I thought that would be a guy but turned out to be a woman. I asked "Hui?" She said "Hui."

I always greet my passengers by their names to show respect and to confirm that they are special enough for me to pay attention to their persona by learning their name even before we get to know each other. Unless I cannot pronounce it, then I ask what their name is.

Chicago is such a diverse city where you can meet people from all over the world. We have so many visitors in one day that other places do not experience in a month!

Therefore, it should not be surprising to meet someone whose name is Dharmeelolar, right?

Well...

When Dharmeelolar enters your small world in the size of a pickup truck's cabin, you can certainly feel how hard your differences are trying to get to know each other.

How about picking up Onanong at Joong Boo market? Wait, what? Where? For a second you forget where you are and who you are...

I have a long list of different names of people that I have met. It was really hard to narrow the list to pick just ten names for the Top Ten Unusual Names.

This list is not to criticize or to make fun of anybody. It is to acknowledge our differences and to celebrate them!

To be completely honest there was only one time, one passenger, when I saw the name, I could not stop myself from wondering how that person lives with such a name. Not sure if that could possibly be a nickname, did not want to bother him asking. Wherever he was going, I wanted to drop him off and forget ever seeing him. Oh, and if you are wondering what his name was—Satan!

I have met Kings and Queens, Babes and Bosses, and Barbies. In most cases one of each. The name Satan was from a different category though (I would even say from a different world), thankfully the only one as well. Just to make it clear—this name is not on the list.

I would like to apologize to everyone who did not make the list. Those would be Michael, John, Jen, Sam, Liz, Peter, Brandon, Stephanie, Brenda, Susan, and Chris. Even Pinqing, Lujia, Berlin, Paris, Zhu, Ajoke, Yiying, Mushfig, Lancelot, Tanker, and many others did not make it. Sorry, cannot comfort you, guys by saying that there will be another list for you too...

Actually, there could be one!

A list of a common personality traits based on the name. At this time, I would like to mention only one name that would top the list—Michael. Of all the people I have met, the ones with the name Michael or Mike are the most down to earth, pleasant, easy to talk to, having the least expectations and demands. Funny. 5 stars!

Alright!

Here is the list of Top Ten Unusual Names that I have had a chance to meet in person their owners:

10. Adegboyega
9. Sucharita
8. Alcibiades
7. Aakanksha
6. ViralkumarDUP
5. Varadarajan
4. Hyunzoo

3. Dharmeelolar

2. Arshdeep

Slowly but steadily we have approached the name that had become the leader of the list of all the unusual names.

Red carpet. Music. Lights.

"And the winner is!"

Louder music, please, to prolong the anticipation!

1."Soontarawadee"

If you would ask me why this name is better than others, the answer would be "It is not better as there are no bad ones!"

It is hard to explain but I still remember the feeling that name gave me. It was like a prediction of the future promising something mysterious and good at the same time. Good because of the energy this person had. Incredibly positive and optimistic.

The name we are given at birth. Are we happy with it? Do we represent the meaning this name includes? In some cultures, there are a whole lot of expectations in connection with the name a person is given—the names of saints, gods, political leaders, TV personalities, actors. What if we do not like our name or the association with the "famous" person our name

119

has? Our parents who named us are from a different generation, but we must live today. What if we do not fit in?

Just as a thought... How about if growing up (let's say at the age of 18) as a part of our development we could change our name based on who WE really are?

Facts

"The impossible is justified by the fact that it occurred."

~ Honoré de Balzac ~

S tatistics, compliments, and badges from my account in the Rideshare app.

4.99-star rating

7320 trips over 2.5 years

Over 3000 Five-star trips

The biggest tip $300. The ride was close to three hours long crossing three states (Illinois, Indiana, and Michigan).

There is a section in the app called "Compliments" where passengers leave comments. They are very important to each driver because their value if they come from the heart is more than any tip can ever cover.

Here are some of them.

* * *

"Thank you so much for the ride home in the rain!

You are absolutely gorgeous and charismatic.

Best of both worlds. Thank you!!!!!!"

* * *

"Thank you for your kind and heartfelt words.

They were incredibly perceptive, and I will carry your

positive thoughts with me in my life."

* * *

"She's the best!"

* * *

"You are amazing! Thank you for the wonderful ride home

(heart)"

* * *

"Thank you so much for an amazing experience"

* * *

*"Wonderful wonderful wonderful ride. Had a very great
conversation that really woke me up! Thank you!"*

* * *

"Thank you for being so nice!"

* * *

"Thank you soooo much girl..."

* * *

*"Thank you for your courteous professionalism and
your warm dialogue."*

* * *

*"Thank you for the enjoyable ride, you're awesome.
10-star service."*

* * *

*"Thank you for the wonderful ride,
I really enjoyed the conversation."*

* * *

*"Thank you for the encouraging words.
Really helped me to figure out a lot."*

* * *

*"Thank you for welcoming me to Chicago from Austin.
Enjoyed your company!"*

* * *

"Thank you again! You made crazy traffic enjoyable. Cheers!"

* * *

*"Best Rideshare of my Life!!! What an amazing person
with a huge heart and so much intuition."*

* * *

"Great driver with a terrific personality"

* * *

"Easily the best Rideshare I've ever had—great person, great conversation and just an overall enjoyable ride."

* * *

"Thank you for your wise words and great conversation. Never thought I'd have a lasting effect from a simple ride. Thank you."

* * *

"First Rideshare ever... She was on time, friendly and professional! Thank you!"

* * *

"Thank you for my first Rideshare!!!!!! You made it very easy for me since I was so nervous. I would ride with you anytime!!!!"

* * *

"Thank you for your positive energy!!! You made my day!"

* * *

"Hey! I just barely caught my flight, thank you so much!"

* * *

"Thanks again! You are a unique driver!"

* * *

"Thank you for being such an awesome ride!! Merry Christmas!"

* * *

"I wish I could've talked more with you but the ride wasn't long enough! You are amazing!"

THANK YOU ALL!

Revisiting and reading this section in my Rideshare account really warmed my heart. I could still recognize most of the people who wrote those notes. They reminded me of all the good times, and made me miss the driving...

If there ever comes the time that I delete my Rideshare driver's app on the phone, this book will always be a reminder of an interesting time with priceless experiences in my life.

To Be Continued...

Made in the USA
Columbia, SC
17 March 2021

34583794R00072